Triple-A Battery

Marie Magnetic

Presentation by *BookLeaf Publishing*

Web: www.bookleafpub.com

E-mail: info@bookleafpub.com

ISBN: 9789357615457

First edition 2022

24 hour rental

bikes and buses pass by my park bench
i'm waiting and watching the throngs
of busy bodies
buzzing like drones
hordes of humans
who are holding something quite heavy
seeking and searching for hollowed-out hives
in tree tops far from here
some people are just here for the ride
and others belong to the journey
some of us forage for our intentions
while others may hunt down desires
eating ambitions as if they were birthday cake
i think by now, i've figured out longing
we all want a taste of that clover honey
but most cannot endure the stings of sorrow
my life has been cobbled together
with spare parts repurposed
i've sifted through bits and pieces
of those i once knew
and those i'll forever love
aware that the roles i play
will always be assorted flavors
when i was a child,
i learned to censor my yearning

never realizing the faults of my foes
match the flaws that i own
displacement means that i never stuck
where others tried to plant me
i thrived in the places that were
unknown and uneasy
some of us decided to dream silently
or in muted colors
as if we aimed to hide from detection
to stave off attention of those who might
wound or mar
afraid that seeking out kinship and kindness
would be met with scars
but how do you filter a soul?
some of us aim to change the world
though not through personal gain
we recognize the needs of the masses are greater
than
what we alone can give
to triumph is to break not only your chains
but those around you
some of us talk about engagement and intent
yet no one speaks about seclusion
to be infested by isolation
complacency runs rampant amongst the masses
platonic love seems so taboo
a desperate attempt to play human
we wash away grit to
display ourselves squeaky-clean

though this is deception
told to confine ourselves to the standards
in movies and magazines
they say art imitates life
but why must we conform to someone else's
perfect?
i seek those who wish to
chain themselves to something greater
a community of compassionate souls
to take time for purpose
those with hearts so full
who can slow down to watch the paint dry
on shelters where we'll store our surplus
harmony
a multitude of mortal multifaceted gems,
diamonds in the rough
it's hard to say,
but i am enough
the hardest lesson i've yet to learn
my worth is already earned
i no longer chase the ghosts
of those who once haunted me

sinkhole of sours

as the day breaks
and the dew drops glisten
into an elixir
of foreboding foresight
i awaken,
disdained in this
feeling of disorientation
i'd rather know elation
yet, i am tongue-tied
though not for
lack of words
i am estranged from
emotion
absent from apathy
deep dreams of
desperation
haunt me
they dance,
daunting and taunting
as if I were prey
hungry humans halt
their happiness
to feed forsaken phantoms
from years missed
and lives passed

apathy is an apparition of
an aching appetite
one that thirsts
for fervor
i search far
and wide
seeking a steady
sanctity
i transpire the journey
of wayward souls
titillating,
spine-tingling
though only in
my mind
can i imagine
an alliance of
affection
my dreams devote
me to dance
alas,
i am an audience of one

decant desperation

there are no words for
a mother in mourning
her cries are
swans' calls
seeking swift shelter
no bonfire can warm her
she floats,
aimlessly
as wayward winds transpire
to annex
all that is stainless,
and wide-eyed
and safe
we sully each strand of sureness
delegating those who wish
to wield walls
of lax laws
as paragons of purview
whilst those who hold tender
the prospects of purpose
the benign benefactors
vying for vicious venom
of the ravenous rabble
are swayed into
submission

as if one could
defeat despair
why must we wield wounds
as weapons?

metempsychosis

what strength has a woman*
to mourn
to breathe
whilst drowning in stupor
of sly, slinking, slander
a clandestine catalyst
simply to bleed is not enough
you must pull from
the underbelly of
buried gold, raw gemstones
such treasured trysts
this stalwart opus will arc
into an evolution of conscience
it will fasten and implant
though it will tangle
in sync
with the mortals
in masse
they may mark you
a firebrand of unpaid candor
but you are not tinder
you are the fire
neither a martyr
nor a souvenir of
delicious ambitions

you own the hammer
you wield the scythe
your heart is
welded sheet metal
tempered to arm your children
with gifts of grandeur
the thirst of justice
will be quenched by flames
we are phoenixes
awaiting ash

*My inclusion of the word 'woman' is meant to
describe my own identity as a cisgender,
bisexual woman, and not to seclude non-binary
or gender non-conforming people.

lurid longing

sweet berries drip languidly
from your lips
the waters of my storm awaken
and within me,
life stirs for the first time
we become entangled in a venus trap
of succulent secrets
this tête-à-tête of
our fruit-bearing labors
will reap both pleasure
and pain
although you dear,
are worth it
you quench my thirst

jazz-fire

steady as an
oak tree
you stand amongst the
forest
content that your role
is to be grounded
from an
ingenious seed
of candor
your branches may sway
though your roots,
in acumen,
sink deeply
while endless
leaves of doubt
dash and dart
far and wide
slipping, sinking
cascading o'er
mountains of
ubiquitous caches
plundering for treasure
but they will never
touch your riches
they will never

hear your truths
as a sapling rises
sky-high
and statuesque
you bask in the
daylight of
gentle giants
and the
nightshade of fierce fervor
you are protector
of wayward souls

hypnopedia

an aching heart,
while fragile,
holds both glory
and shame
feathers plucked
from decayed matter
float aimlessly
as if they have lost
their internal compass
instincts are shattered
and shorn
thought we are not
sheep of shame
we amble past roaring waters,
longing for languid lochs
reaching out for comfort
uncertain of the journey
though we own
the ships of serendipity
grains of sand
won't budge this windmill
we gather in secret
questioning not the tides,
but those who aim to barricade
the gifts of nature

they wish to own
the skies, the seas
in absence of conscience
wearing away mountains
as if they were
volcanic ash
seeking a land
devoid of fruit and flower
ambiguously serving time
to flora and fauna
as the hourglass fades
into the background
merely pawns
in the chess game
of life
our cocoons
obscure
bits of the
common strife

hourglass of seconds

the minute hand
strikes sorrow
each tick dreads its turn
in passing time
supple, sticky, swamps
of molasses
dredge us in monotony
a sinking swan dive
sweeps in strange secrets
i've been here once a fortnight
thick, fleshed-out cores
of raw, wrinkled, wishes
jack-o-lanterns
stored in bureaus
of burning bridges
before we've built them
gusty, gloomy, gales
of grief-
gasping, gleaning
wretched hearts
are weak to plunder,
wary to slumber
one dolorous dance
in the doorstep-
a misstep
how do you sacrifice shame?

deep-fried pine wood

your darkness runs
down the walls
like waterfalls
trickling,
aerating a sensation
of complacent
elation
though a deep,
destructive sickness
burns bridges
it follows you
blindly
with visions almighty
woe is me,
cried the sandman
a creature whose
broken plans
to save us
from the thick
brush
are absconded
when will justice
reach us?

decant desperation

there are no words for
a mother in mourning
her cries are
swans' calls
seeking swift shelter
no bonfire can warm her
she floats,
aimlessly
as wayward winds transpire
to annex
all that is stainless,
and wide-eyed
and safe
we sully each strand of sureness
delegating those who wish
to wield walls
of lax laws
as paragons of purview
whilst those who hold tender
the prospects of purpose
the benign benefactors
vying for vicious venom
of the ravenous rabble
are swayed into
submission

as if one could
defeat despair
why must we wield wounds
as weapons?

days of de novo

i never saw the sunlight until i decided
to shine
just waiting for someone
to brighten my life
only made days darker
and nights clamor
to claim my solace
i've held onto many
babbling baubles
battling and brawling
to lessen the blows
i won't quell my nature
to secure your stupor
we all long for connection
and candor
but this network runs on
the complacency
of foolish folk
who've halted hope

savoring the sculpture

love is raw
your hands,
they knead and press my folds
into a dough
of delightful
dalliance
you plant seeds
that will grow
a garden
of delectable dreams
i watch and
wait patiently
as you mold
my smudges
into morsels
only you will
devour

ephemeron

21

within these tempestuous towers
whatever we grow, flowers
and in these april showers
your fate and fortune glowers
if humankind lulls, cowers
discerns its righteous powers
the ticking clock bends hours

garibaldi park

if i plant my roots here
cement myself to the earth
i notice that
while i am safe
from tempest winds
whose aim is to lift
and shake
and ravage my insides
this heavenly haven
has clipped my wings
the surety and safeness
of fertilized ground
begets poison
and though i seek
to germinate seeds
sunlight cannot reach me
in the shade
of solitude

sandwich cookie

mundane secrets
make each moment vibrant
colored with the cloth
of discarded daydreams
our roles are unabating
in losing, we gain
we slumber in pain

iowa

24

corn crops confine cunning crowds
folks flee from forsaken feelings
they trudge tirelessly through thick terrain
refusing reflective rhetoric
only opposing our own opulence
arguing absurd, antagonistic authority
above altruistic aid
humanity holds hollow

guarding the gutter

25

you breathe in raindrops
trickling,
tittering
into abundance
you wash off your
wind wings
of wonder

golden rings

a storm's a-brewin'
and i can see the eye
sanctity of my safehouse
tarnishes with time
all light has dulled
peace neutralized
to pay my dues
as a martyr of dimes